# Table of Contents

## Dedicated

to my sons,
Mark, Daren, and Brent
who, with much love, continue to
teach me how to manage conflicts
and

to my nephew,
Reid,
who, at age sixteen,
is illustrating his first book

Educational Media Corporation®

# Introduction

Hi! Welcome to *Conflict Resolution and Mediation for Peer Helpers*. No doubt we have come together because we share an interest in helping others to cope with conflicts. For nearly two decades it has been my pleasure to be part of an exciting and innovative educational program—the peer helper movement.

The concept of people helping people is not new. However, the idea of providing systematic training in communication and helping skills for young people is. Since the mid 70s, a variety of peer helper programs have sprung up across the country.

Different names are used—peer facilitators, peer counselors, PALs, or friendly helpers, to name a few. All are united in the common purpose of equipping young people to provide timely assistance to others.

These programs contain components for understanding human behavior, for learning communication skills, and for solving problems.

One pioneer program features a developmental approach to helping. In this program peer helpers are viewed as "facilitators." Using the facilitative model developed by Robert D. Myrick and Joe Wittmer of the University of Florida, peer facilitators learn to function in four basic roles: small group leader, big brother/big sister, special friend, and tutor.

The first training materials centered on this approach were published in 1978. *Caring and Sharing: Becoming a Peer Facilitator* (student book) and *Youth Helping Youth: A Handbook for Training Peer Facilitators* (leader's manual) were both co-authored by counselor educator Robert D. Myrick and then high school counselor Tom Erney. These materials continue to be viable for training peer helpers.

Through the years peer helping has become a major resource for combating many problems confronting youth. As the programs grow, additional components are added to the training.

In 1991 Robert D. Myrick again teamed up with a counselor and peer helper trainer, Betsy E. Folk. The result was *Peervention: Training Peer Facilitators for Prevention Education*, a student handbook, and the accompanying leader's manual, *The Power of Peervention*. In addition to providing the materials necessary for teaching basic helping and responding skills, this program features activities and suggestions for involving peer helpers in ten areas of prevention education.

The list of projects peer helpers are being asked to perform expands each year. Conflict resolution and mediation are some of the newer tasks being undertaken by peer helpers. Although we are making progress promoting tolerance for people of different backgrounds and beliefs, when we interact with a variety of people, conflicts invariably result.

Stepping into the middle of a conflict is serious business. It should be undertaken with great care after thorough preparation, to avoid negative consequences to those involved, including the peer helpers.

*Conflict Resolution and Mediation for Peer Helpers* is not intended to be a complete training program. It is designed to provide supplemental information to other peer training programs such as *Caring and Sharing/Youth Helping Youth* and *Peervention*.

We will begin by looking at conflicts and how to manage and resolve them. We will close with a systematic procedure for mediating the conflicts of others.

# Part I

# Conflict Resolution

# 1

# Internal and External Conflicts

*"Friday nights used to be fun. Life was simpler last year. Nobody had a car so we all just hung out at the mall. If we had money, we went to a movie. Everybody seemed to get along. Now, there are so many hassles. Some of my old friends are into things that I don't want to do. It seems like we are always arguing."*

Although conflicts are an inevitable part of living, caring people have long sought ways to lessen the negative impact of conflicts. Most people can easily recognize when they or others are in conflict. However, they often have trouble coping with controversy because they don't understand the nature of conflicts and they lack the interpersonal skills necessary to deal with them.

First we will attempt to understand the nature of conflicts, then we will look at some strategies for managing and resolving them.

Conflicts build both *within* us and *outside* of us.

*Internal* **conflicts** result when opposing forces— our drives or desires—demand that we do something to provide satisfaction.

> *"I want to go skiing this weekend, but I know I'll be pretty tired after the basketball game Friday night."*

*External* **conflicts** result because we must live in a world with others. Our needs and values sometimes conflict with the needs and values of others.

> *"I know I told you I would help you with your science project this weekend, but my mom is working and I have to stay home and take care of my little brother."*

Educational Media Corporation®

## Internal Conflicts

The founder of psychoanalysis, Sigmund Freud, provided a useful model for understanding the nature of many *internal* conflicts.

Briefly, Freud suggested that at birth we are dominated by a portion of our mind which he called the *id*, the seat of our passions and impulses. When we are hungry, the id demands food. When we are tired, the id demands sleep. Internal conflicts can occur when we have two or more competing tensions to be reduced. The id strives to reduce tension and to experience pleasure. When the impulses of the *id* are firmly in control, we might say that the person is *impulsive*.

> *"I was on the way to the bowling alley. I had planned to go bowling. But, as I drove by the theatre, I decided I wanted to see this movie—now!"*

It is the task of another portion of our mind, the *ego*, to interact with external reality (our environment) to obtain from the world what we need. The ego helps us to either adjust to the demands of the world and delay gratification or it enables us to take the necessary action to master our environment and to satisfy our needs and drives. When the *ego* is firmly in control, we might say that the person is *realistic*.

> *"Kim Lee is so practical. She always checks the prices before she decides anything. I don't think she has ever done anything just for the fun of it. Everything has to have a purpose."*

Freud suggested that there was a third portion of the mind which he labeled the *super ego*. It represents the ideal rather than the real, and it strives for perfection rather than for reality or pleasure. Before we could reason for ourselves, our conception of what our parents considered to be morally good was established in a part of the super ego called the *ego ideal*. The other portion of the super ego, the *conscience*, developed as we learned what our parents and society believed to be morally bad or evil. There can be internal conflicts *within* the super ego between the ego ideal and the conscience. When the super ego is firmly in control, we might say that the person is *moralistic*.

> *"It just wouldn't be right to do it. I know nobody would find out, but I just can't do it."*

The healthy individual is one where the impulsive, realistic, and moralistic components of personality are in balance with each other. The ego, in its role as mediator, intervenes in conflicts *within* and *between* the other sub-parts of the mind. Since internal conflicts reside within us, it is within our power alone to resolve them. Sometimes, however, we can benefit from sharing our feelings and desires with someone who cares enough to listen to our internal conflicts without condemning, evaluating, or judging us.

We will spend the majority of the book learning about external conflicts—conflicts between people.

## External Conflicts

External conflicts exist whenever incompatible things happen *between* people. When there are *differences* in information, beliefs, opinions, assumptions, ideas, needs, values, and goals, conflicts exist.

> *"Everyone knows the school colors are red and blue. Why would anyone want green band uniforms?"*

Conflicts also result when there are *shortages* of certain resources such as time, space, money, power, influence, and position.

> *"I want to go in the morning, but Shannon isn't a morning person. He wants to leave at noon. I know we won't see it all before it closes."*

*Competitions* or rivalries also produce conflicts. When you are in competition, your goals are in opposition to the goals of the others. You want to win, which means you want your competitor to lose.

> *"It's not fair to give the class that sells the most pizzas a day off from school. The seniors have more cars and can get around better."*

*Cooperation* can also foster conflict. You can disagree about the best way to achieve goals you both share. Your parents may be in agreement in the desire to raise you to become a caring and responsible adult, but they may not always agree on the best way to accomplish this.

Conflicts are inevitable, even in the friendliest of groups. They are a natural and desirable part of any relationship. A conflict is a moment of truth, a test of a relationship. Conflicts can weaken or strengthen relationships. They are critical events that can bring creative insight and closer relationships, or lasting resentment. Conflicts can push us away from each other or pull us into closer and more cooperative relationships. They may result in aggression or mutual understanding.

Conflicts sometimes occur because we make some false assumptions about others. We should not assume that others are always completely informed about all aspects of a situation. A conflict may result from a lack of information.

It is also not appropriate to assume that others will always be sensitive to our needs and feelings. While we would like to believe that others demonstrate a reasonable amount of sensitivity and caring, they may be blinded by their own needs and desires.

Humans are capable of rational thought, but it would be false to assume that others always think and act rationally. Irrational behavior can occur when we least expect it.

We should be careful not to avoid conflicts or to resolve them too soon. We need to explore our differences to better understand ourselves and others. From conflicts emerge the best—or the worst—in us.

## Summary

Internal conflicts result when opposing forces within us demand gratification at the same time. External conflicts result when our needs and values conflict with the needs and values of others. These conflicts result when there are differences between people and when there are shortages of certain resources.

If we want a better, safer world, it has to start with us—with our daily interactions with others. In chapter 2 we will explore some additional sources of external conflicts.

## Activities/Discussion

1. How do you generally react to situations? Are you primarily *impulsive* (id-dominated), *realistic* or *practical* (ego-dominated), or *moralistic* (superego-dominated)?

2. Give an example of an *internal* conflict and describe how you would respond.

3. Do most of your *external* conflicts result from a *shortage of resources* or *differences* with others?

4. What might you do to reduce your conflicts with others that result from *shortages*?

5. What might you do to reduce your conflicts with others that result from *differences* of values, and so forth?

6. Have you experienced an unhealthy conflict with someone that resulted from a *rivalry* or *competition?* What might you do to reduce these unhealthy conflicts?

7. Five members of your training group have a cooperative assignment. Each of you will receive an envelope containing several odd shapes of paper. Each is to construct a six-inch square under the following rules: a) *No* talking, pointing, or signaling; b) You may not *ask for* or *take* a piece from someone else: c) You may *give* puzzle pieces to others. Observe the behavior of the group members as they work toward their common goal of completing five individual squares. (Instructions for the trainer are provided on page 126.)

# 2

# Additional Source of External Conflicts

*"We tried, but we just couldn't agree. We don't seem to have anything in common."*

Conflicts with others are a natural part of our everyday lives. Whenever people live, work, or play together, conflicts also occur because of *honest perceptual differences, misunderstandings, irritations, inappropriate expectations,* and *unknown sources.*

## Honest Perceptual Differences

Whenever two or more people are gathered together, differences in perception are bound to occur. These differences often lead to conflicts.

Look at the illustration below. What do you see?

If you saw the white figure against a black background, then you saw a vase. If you saw the black figures against a white background, then you saw two human profiles facing each other. You can see one or the other, but you cannot see both *at the same time*. Now that you are aware of both objects, you can *choose* which one you wish to give your attention to at the moment.

          Educational Media Corporation®

Here is another example of how various people can view the same object differently. Look at this picture. Do you see a young girl or an old woman?

What made the difference? Look at picture A and picture B on the following page.

A                                    B

If you were to see picture A first and then look at the picture on the previous page, you no doubt would see the young girl. However, if you were to see picture B first, you would probably see the old woman in the composite picture. *Previous experiences* tend to influence how we perceive things.

For some of us our perceptions are altered by *genetic differences*. People who are color blind definitely perceive some things differently from those of us who are not. Differences in perceptions will always exist because of inherent differences in our genetic and experiential backgrounds.

*"I was brought up in the country where we never locked anything. My girlfriend has been a city girl all her life. She locks everything. It sure is frustrating to be searching for keys all the time."*

We are products of our environments, of our ancestry, and of our experiences. Twin siblings growing up in the same household still have different experiences. Their parents have no difficulty recognizing the differences in their personalities. Each twin has a different way of perceiving the world, and conflicts between them will inevitably result.

For a conflict to be experienced, it first must be perceived. Two people who fail to notice or acknowledge their incompatibility will not be in conflict with each other. Everyday we interact with others with whom we find little in common, but we choose not to enter into conflicts with them.

Sometimes incomparability is perceived when it doesn't exist. Prejudices reinforce perceived incompatibility as we choose to react to negative stereotypes rather than to the actual person. If we really got to know the other person, we probably would find that we have more in common than we realize. Perceived incompatibility arouses anger. However, it also can provide motivation for change.

## Misunderstandings

Even if two people perceive a situation similarly, conflicts can result because of misunderstandings—failures to communicate.

Understanding is an important ingredient in positive relationships. It creates a certain degree of predictability which is invaluable for maintaining relationships. When we understand one another, the chances of a conflict are reduced.

Misunderstanding is a major contributor to relationship problems. The loneliest people in the world are usually people who are frequently misunderstood. Feelings of disappointment, anger, and loneliness are associated with chronic misunderstanding.

**Disclosure.** Misunderstandings often result when we fail to disclose information about ourselves, or when we fail to encourage disclosure in others.

*"I really would like to know how you feel about me. I have come to admire you very much and I would like to get to know you better."*

When the other person does not know about our feelings and thoughts, we increase the chances of being misunderstood. When we do not encourage others to disclose, misunderstandings also are likely to result.

Understanding requires that information be *mutually* disclosed. With only partial disclosure comes partial understanding. Others must guess about what is going on inside us, and we must guess what is going on inside others.

Educational Media Corporation®

**Faulty assumptions.** Actions taken that are based on assumptions or guesses can lead to misunderstanding.

> *"I didn't think you cared about me. I told Ricky that I would go out with him Friday night. I was angry with you because you didn't call me."*

Misunderstanding can also result when we assume that once something has been said, it has been understood. A basic error in communication comes from the assumption that words mean the same to all people. Although most people share roughly the same meaning for many words, always check out your assumptions with the person who is speaking.

**Denotations and connotations.** Words have both *denotations* and *connotations* .

*Denotations* are the direct, explicit meanings or references of a word or a term. We generally understand what is meant when we use the words table, chair, person, house, and so forth. We know what the words represent or denote.

> *"Please bring the packages from the car into the house."*

There is not too much chance to misunderstand what is *denoted* in this message. There are *packages* in the *car* and they are to be brought into the *house*.

However, the *connotations* of a word are the ideas suggested by or associated with a word *in addition to* its explicit meaning or denotation. It is in the connotations that confusion in communication results. What a word *connotes* can vary from person to person. We need to check to be sure that a word or phase connotes the same thing to us, the listener, that it did to the speaker.

Let us look at the previous example:

*"Please bring the packages from the car into the house (now)."*

By the tone of voice of the speaker, we might infer that assistance is politely requested. The speaker probably wants the assistance *now*. If the listener chooses to interpret the message as a task that can be done *at any time,* a conflict may result. Good communicators will remain alert to the possibilities that misunderstandings can and do occur.

**Feelings.** In this conflict resolution model, we are presenting some basic communication skills designed to reduce misunderstandings. Many of life's conflicts can be avoided it we simply "tune in" to what the other person is experiencing, paying special attention to the *feelings* that accompany the words that are being spoken.

> *"When your coach gets on your case and stays there, you feel embarrassed. You get angry when he picks on you. Sometimes you even think about quitting."*

Feelings *energize* our behaviors. Have you noticed that as your feelings intensify, your desire to act on those feelings increases?

> *"Sometimes I get so angry that I can hardly control myself."*

If you are unaware of your feelings, you may lack the energy to take action. Important steps to conflict resolution are to become aware of your feelings and to decide what action you want to take as a result of those feelings.

# Irritations

People hurt each other all the time. Sometimes the behavior of another results in our experiencing *unpleasant* feelings. These irritating feelings produce discomfort within us. We need to share our unpleasant feelings with the person with whom we are in conflict in a way that will produce a constructive outcome. We need to learn to give *feedback* to another concerning how that person's behavior is affecting us.

> *"When you leave our locker door open, that really irritates me. Sometimes I think I should go to the office and have them assign a different locker partner."*

Before giving *negative* feedback to another, take sufficient time to build a relationship with that person so your feedback will be accepted. Care should be exercised to give negative feedback only when it is concerns something significant.

When the situation merits, the feedback given should concern a *specific* behavior. Tell how that *behavior* makes you *feel*, and what *you* are considering doing as a result of *your feelings*. Do not label or judge the other person, or tell that person what to do.

Educational Media Corporation®

## Inappropriate Expectations

Psychologist Fritz Perls once said, "I am not in this world to please you and you are not in this world to please me...." If we would believe this and take it to heart, we would be freed from a major source of conflicts—inappropriate expectations of each other. It is not rational to expect that everyone in this world will like us, or that we can live up to all of the expectations that others have for us.

> *"My mom always wanted me to become an Eagle Scout. I couldn't stand the Boy Scouts, but I stayed in it for six years. Mom was always setting goals for me that I didn't want to achieve!"*

Perfectionism is serious and disabling. We are imperfect beings in an imperfect world. We need to accept some failings and shortcomings in others and in ourselves. This does not mean that we should not strive for excellence; it is good to take joy from a job well done. Much has been accomplished by people who are willing to give maximum effort for a good cause. However, mistakes will be made because we are human. These errors, if not forgiven, can contribute to the destruction of something very precious—a human being.

# Unknown Sources

We have pointed to some sources of external conflicts. However obvious the sources of many conflicts may be, the source of some conflicts may never be known to anyone. Sometimes it is useful to know the source or reason for the conflict; other times that information is of little or no use.

*"As long as I can remember, I have been fighting with the guy next door. We never seemed to agree about anything. Maybe it was just a personality conflict. Well, it doesn't matter any more. He moved away."*

It is not necessary to assess blame in order to resolve a conflict. Knowing who or what began the conflict does not necessarily aid in resolving it.

# Summary

External conflicts occur because of honest perceptual differences, misunderstandings, irritations, inappropriate expectations, and unknown sources. We differ in our perceptions of the world because of our genetic and experiential backgrounds.

Failures in communication can result in misunderstandings. Learning to identify and to clarify feelings is one way to reduce misunderstandings.

Things other people say and do can irritate us. When appropriate, feedback given to others can help them to understand how their behavior is affecting us.

The expectations of others often conflict with our own desires and needs. Freeing ourselves from these expectations enables us to set our own goals and to make our own decisions. It is not necessary to assess blame in order to resolve a conflict.

Often the answer to resolving a conflict lies inside ourselves. In chapter 3 we will take a look inside ourselves at our feelings and our psychological needs.

## Activities/Discussion

1. What strong feelings or values have you acquired as a result of you childhood experiences? How do your feelings and values differ from those of your brother(s) or sister(s)?

2. Reflect on a time when you were misunderstood by someone. Did you try to "set that person straight?" If so, what did you do to communicate your correct feelings or ideas?

3. Is there someone who repeatedly does something that irritates you? Practice giving feedback to that person concerning how a *specific* behavior affects you. Tell that person what *you* are considering doing as a result of *your feelings* about the other's behavior.

4. Do you sometimes try to live up to the expectations someone else has for you? Give an example of such an expectation. Does that person's expectation conflict with your own desires? How do you plan to resolve this conflict?

# 3

# Looking Inside Ourselves

*"If Jeremy wasn't so stubborn, I wouldn't be in trouble now. I wanted to leave earlier, but he insisted on staying. I didn't have any way to get home by myself."*

It is much easier to place the blame for conflicts on others or on circumstances. Looking within and discovering our own responsibility for conflicts goes against our basic human nature. However, the process of resolving our conflicts with others begins by looking within ourselves.

## Meeting Our Psychological Needs

Although there are certain basic physical and physiological needs that we must meet (food, air, water, and body temperature), much of our behavior is directed toward satisfying certain basic *psychological* **needs**. What we do often is directed to the task of satisfying these needs. Among those psychological needs are the needs to be loved and accepted, to feel secure, *to belong.*

> *"Do you know what he dared me to do? He dared me to wait until class started and then walk into Ms. Andrews' room and sit down in the front row. No way, man. I don't belong in her class."*

Also, we need to experience a sense of personal *power,* to achieve, to accomplish, and to be recognized and respected for who we are and what we have done.

> *"I want to make a difference. It is not enough just to be accepted, I want people to remember me."*

*Freedom* is also a basic psychological need. We need to feel free—to feel we are in charge of the decisions in our lives.

> *"I know I am just one person, but I can make a difference. I am responsible for my decisions. Sure, there are some decisions I can't make, but no one can control how I feel about what is happening."*

We are pleasure-seeking creatures. We need to have *fun*—to enjoy all that life has to offer. We are motivated to increase the frequency of pleasant experiences in our lives and to decrease the frequency of unpleasant events.

When we successfully achieve our goals and meet our psychological needs, we feel good about ourselves.

*"I choose life. I plan to enjoy life—every day. Sure, there are some things I have to do that aren't pleasant, but I do them so I can enjoy other things. I'd rather have a job that is fun than to work all day at a dull job."*

## The Impact of Feelings on Behavior

How we feel about ourselves is important. People who act out or are withdrawn from others usually do not feel good about themselves. When we feel at peace within ourselves, we can relate to others more effectively. When we feel unworthy, inadequate, or troubled, these feelings will affect the way we deal with and perceive others. Giving in to feelings of hopelessness renders us powerless.

*"I don't care what you think. Nobody has ever done anything for me, so why should I try?"*

Feeling good about ourselves is a first step to relating positively with others.

## Identifying Feelings

Our society has a history of repressing feelings. There is a general myth that to be "objective" and "rational" is to rule out all feelings and emotions. Being objective and rational really means that we utilize all available information in making a decision. Feelings are an important source of information.

Everyone has feelings. When we express ourselves, our ideas are always complimented by feelings, either pleasant, unpleasant, or both.

When others listen to us—and we listen to others—often only the spoken words are heard and the feelings that also are communicated are missed. Feelings are a natural part of our lives and should not be ignored. Some feelings may be easily identified because they were referred to when the story was being told.

*"I am really **upset** because nothing was done while I was away. It **hurts** to have my instructions ignored."*

Other feelings are found behind the words. They may be a driving force or an emotional expression that completes the thoughts and ideas.

*"What am I supposed to do when nobody tells me anything? How can I do my job?"*

## Listening for Feelings

It is important to listen to a person with whom you have a conflict. Knowing and understanding how the other person feels is important to determining that person's needs and desires.

A practical way to be aware of the feelings of others is to ask, "Am I hearing *pleasant* or *unpleasant* feelings? Or am I hearing *both* kinds of feelings?" This little technique will help you to focus your attention on what the other person is experiencing. It also gives you a hint as to how you might respond.

Think of different situations in your everyday life. Try to imagine the feelings that you expect would be present. For instance, suppose that someone noticed that your car had a scratch in its new paint job and told you about it. What if you worked on a class project for several hours more than you expected and you were still not finished? How might you feel in these situations? What are some typical kinds of feelings that might be present, both pleasant and unpleasant?

## Expanding Your Vocabulary

It is important to be able to identify a variety of pleasant and unpleasant feelings. Expanding your vocabulary of feeling words helps you to be more sensitive to your own feelings and to the feelings of others. A list of some pleasant and unpleasant feeling words follows to assist you in this task.

# Unpleasant Feelings Words

Abandoned
Agony
Ambivalent
Angry
Annoyed
Anxious
Betrayed
Bitter
Bored
Burdened
Cheated
Cold
Condemned
Confused
Crushed
Defeated
Despair
Destructive
Different
Diminished
Discontented
Distracted

Distraught
Disturbed
Dominated
Divided
Dubious
Empty
Envious
Exasperated
Exhausted
Fatigued
Fearful
Flustered
Foolish
Frantic
Frustrated
Frightened
Grief
Guilty
Intimidated
Irritated
Isolated
Jealous

Left Out
Lonely
Longing
Low
Mad
Maudlin
Mean
Melancholy
Miserable
Nervous
Odd
Overwhelmed
Pain
Panicked
Persecuted
Petrified
Pity
Pressured
Quarrelsome
Rejected
Remorse
Restless

Sad
Scared
Shocked
Skeptical
Sorrowful
Startled
Strained
Stupid
Stunned
Tenuous
Tense
Threatened
Tired
Trapped
Troubled
Uneasy
Unsettled
Vulnerable
Weak
Weepy
Worried

# Pleasant Feeling Words

Adequate
Affectionate
Befriended
Bold
Calm
Capable
Caring
Challenged
Charmed
Cheerful
Clever
Comforting
Confident
Content

Delighted
Determined
Eager
Ecstatic
Enchanted
Enhanced
Energetic
Enervated
Enjoyed
Excited
Fascinated
Fearless
Free
Fulfilled

Generous
Glad
Gratified
Groovy
Happy
Helpful
High
Honored
Important
Impressed
Infatuated
Inspired
Joyful
Kind
Loving

Loved
Peaceful
Pleasant
Pleased
Proud
Refreshed
Relaxed
Relieved
Rewarded
Safe
Satisfied
Secure
Settled
Sure
Warm

Educational Media Corporation®

## Acknowledging the Feelings of Others

When you attempt to resolve a conflict, it is important to listen to what the other person is saying and to identify the feelings being expressed. You need to let the other person know you understand what is being shared. Do this by summarizing the content and by identifying the feelings you are hearing. Restate what you have heard. Be sure to include feeling words in your restatement.

> *"I enjoy my job, but what am I supposed to do when nobody tells me anything? How can I do my job?"*

What feelings are you hearing? There is a pleasant feeling: "I *enjoy* my job," but there is also an unpleasant feeling that is implied: *frustration* at not knowing what to do.

Let the other person know you are aware of the feelings by placing the feeling words in a sentence.

> *"Although you **enjoy** your job, you are **frustrated** by not knowing what to do. It is **discouraging** to not be able to function as you would like."*

Don't be afraid to make an *educated* guess at the feelings that are *implied* by the words of the other person. If you demonstrate by listening that you are really interested in *understanding* the other person, that person undoubtedly will correct you if the feeling words you have chosen are inaccurate.

By listening to and identifying the feelings of others, you demonstrate how you would like others to respond to you. Becoming aware of each others needs, desires, and feelings provides a good foundation for conflict resolution.

## Summary

Resolving conflicts begins by looking within ourselves. Our behavior is directed toward satisfying certain basic psychological needs, i.e., the need to belong, to experience power, and to be free to make choices that will permit us to enjoy life.

Feelings and behaviors are closely related. To relate positively with others, we must first feel good about ourselves. Feelings are an important source of information about the needs, wants, and desires of people in conflict.

Like so many other things in our lives, we are free to choose how we feel. Managing conflicts requires that we have a good understanding of how we make choices. In chapter 4 we will explore the process of choosing.

## Activities/Discussion

1. What *psychological* need is the strongest in your life at this time (belonging, power, freedom, or fun)? What are some of the ways you are using to gratify that need?

2. Select a current situation in your life for which you have some strong feelings. Share that situation with another person or with the group. Permit the listener or the group to identify the feelings you are expressing.

3. "Brainstorm" words that describe *pleasant* feelings. List as many of these words as possible for all to see. Then, "brainstorm" words that describe *unpleasant* feelings. Which list was longer? Which list was easier to make? What are some of the reasons for this?

# 4

# The Process of Choosing

> *"I liked to procrastinate. It seemed that some unpleasant things went away if I waited long enough. Then I noticed that some good things also disappeared if I waited. I decided to take more control of my life—to make my own choices and to quit procrastinating."*

Conflicts are the inevitable outcomes of our ability to make choices. We have no alternative. We *must* make choices. If we are confronted with a choice and we do not make it, in reality *we have chosen* not to choose. As one psychologist put it, we are *condemned* to choice. There is no avoiding choice in our lives.

It is in our best interests to fully understand the art of choosing—to learn how to make enlightened, intelligent choices from an ever broadening range of alternatives.

## Choosing the Best Alternative

In helping others to resolve conflicts, it is useful to assume that *each person,* consciously or otherwise, *is always making the best choice available at the time.* These individuals are operating from models or representations of the world that they have created. Their personal maps or models contain a *limited* range of choices. Any limitations they might experience are typically the result of the *model* of the world *they* have *created* and not the world itself.

> *"I had a hard time understanding that the real world was greater than my understanding of it. If I was having trouble making good choices, it was not because there were no good alternatives available. It was because I was not aware of other alternatives."*

Conflict resolution often requires that we learn how to expand our models of the world to broaden our range of choices. We also need to become more aware of the consequences of our choices. When we choose, we are either choosing life or death, good or evil.

## Opposites and the Opposition

Whether our present circumstances are pleasant or unpleasant, generally they are the consequences of choices. Many of the choices in our lives are between diametrically opposing forces.

To understand this concept, please complete the following exercise:

| light | dark |
|-------|------|
| night | day  |
| tall  | ____ |
| old   | ____ |
| good  | ____ |

No doubt you said short was the opposite of tall and young the opposite of old. The opposite of good is bad, or evil. Evil seeks to prevent or oppose that which is good in life.

> *"I often hear people say, 'I like you but I don't like what you did.' I wonder what makes good people do bad things?"*

For the majority of us, our *intentions* are to pursue the good life, to avoid evil, and to live at peace with ourselves and others. So, what goes wrong in so many cases? Why is there so much that is bad, evil, and painful in life?

This may be hard for some to accept, but evil often is present because we have *chosen* evil over good. We sometimes make choices without fully understanding the implications of our choices. What we may perceive to be a good choice, may in effect represent a choice for evil.

*"I never gave it much thought. What harm could there be in it? I thought we were just having a little harmless fun. It sure didn't turn out like I thought it would."*

The opposite of life is death. When someone chooses suicide as an alternative for life, it is clear that death was chosen over life. But to many people, choosing to drink a few beers is not clearly seen as a choice of death over life. At first we experience consequences perceived as pleasant, but when the evening turns tragic as an auto accident takes a life, it becomes clearer that the choice to drink was really a choice for death.

*"She wouldn't listen to me. She wanted me to be perfect, like my brother. She was always comparing me to him. I wasn't like him. I didn't see any way things would change, so I tried to kill myself."*

We need to make more enlightened choices by becoming aware of the many life-giving alternatives open to us.

Educational Media Corporation®

## Making Enlightened Choices

To make enlightened choices, follow three simple steps:

1. **Examine the alternatives.** You cannot examine *all* alternatives, but you can make a commitment to always look at more than two possible solutions to any problem or dilemma. Think of as many alternatives as possible by "brainstorming."

2. **Evaluate the consequences of each alternative.** Decide what good would result from each possibility. Then, take the blinders off and look for the negative consequences for each alternative. Weigh the advantages and disadvantages of each option.

3. **Make a choice.** Remembering that not choosing is a choice in itself, take charge of the situation by making the best choice that you can with the information available to you at the moment. An old saying, "A journey of a thousand miles begins with a single step," conveys the message that once you have determined the direction of your journey, get on with it. Make a decision—take a risk and get started toward your goal.

## Choosing and Stress

Making a decision—choosing—produces some psychological stress. Resolving a conflict requires that we make choices. Sometimes we avoid making choices because we become aware of the costs—the risks—involved. The more pessimistic we become about the chances of finding a better alternative, the more unlikely we will seek a solution.

Even though the current situation may be producing considerable stress, we may avoid making changes. It takes time to explore alternatives and to evaluate consequences. If we believe that there is not enough time to find a viable alternative, our stress level also will rise. Instead of seeking a solution, we may continue our present course of action because it seems less risky than any new alternative.

Some people panic at the need to find a solution. They jump at the first alternative offered without evaluating the consequences. They believe that any alternative has got to be better than the way things are. They focus only on the good and ignore the negative aspects of the new opportunity.

People who see serious risk in choosing any of the available alternatives may choose to avoid making a decision. The result is usually pessimism, sarcasm, or depression. Those who postpone a decision—who wait until a later time to decide—secretly hope that the need to choose will disappear. Some who fail to act displace the responsibility for the conflict or the solution on others. They pass the buck, insisting that it is someone else's responsibility to act.

If a conflict produces too much stress, there is a high rate of vacillation—panic—with little productive effort being taken to resolve the situation. If there is too little stress present, there is no motivation to take action. Conflict and stress are interrelated. An appropriate amount of stress is necessary to motivate us to want to make a choice—to resolve the conflict.

## The Absence of Conflict

Conflict can be constructive. We need to be faced with controversies which challenge us to make choices. The absence of conflict can signal disinterest and alienation. While we do not usually actively seek controversy or conflict, we should possess sufficient skills for responding in constructive ways when we are confronted with them.

## Summary

We are constantly making choices—choices which are ultimately choices for good or evil, life or death. Enlightened choices are choices that are made after a careful review of the alternatives and the consequences of each alternative. We then make the best choice available from our own models of the world. In chapter 5 we will look at a variety of ways people respond to conflicts.

## Activities/Discussion

1. Identify a choice you made recently that you believed was a good or life-giving choice that turned out to have unpleasant consequences. Could you have foreseen this development at the time you made the choice? How?

2. Identity a conflict in your life that is currently unresolved. List the alternative solutions available and the consequences of each. Commit to acting on the appropriate solution and report on the outcome.

3. How would you go about expanding your model of the world in a particular area of current concern?

# 5

# Responding to Conflicts

*"It sounded like a great idea. I could work three nights a week from eight until closing. The car payments would be only $149.00 a month. I didn't realize how hard it would be to get my homework done. Dad said he'd pay for the insurance, but I forgot about tires, oil changes, and repairs. Then the transmission went out. I don't have money to fix it and I still have to make the payments. I can't use the car and I'm working to make the payments instead of getting my homework done. What a mess!"*

Conflicts are often approached with confusion. We deal with conflicts constantly, sometimes well, sometimes badly. We are not always aware of our options, so we use strategies that are probably not appropriate for the situation. *It is not the presence of conflicts that causes disastrous and unfortunate things, it is the harmful and ineffective management of conflicts.*

## Managing Conflicts Ineffectively

The consequences of inept or inappropriate conflict management can be severe. Friends can be lost, the joy of a day destroyed, or a relationship damaged when it might have been strengthened. Poor conflict management can affect our own social-emotional growth. When we have managed conflicts badly, we will not risk moving on to richer social experiences.

If we do not accept conflicts or prepare for them, we will be surprised each time they occur. We will respond to conflicts with the same few, limited strategies. We will be unaware of our options. We will not be able to utilize the concept of alternative strategies.

When we are not prepared to deal with conflicts, a conflict will happen to us and we will react quickly, emotionally, and with little consideration of the consequences.

Educational Media Corporation®

# Responding with Violence or Avoidance

Many young people believe that violence and running away are the only ways they have of dealing with conflicts. In choosing violence, they attempt to define conflicts as a *win/lose* propositions. When the choice is running away or avoidance, the conflict is defined as a *lose/win* situation. As we will discuss later, effective conflict resolution requires that we perceive conflicts as *win/win* situations.

**Violence.** Aggressive individuals who use verbal and physical violence can become closed to other alternatives. They lose their ability to recognize when their behavior inflames the conflict rather than resolves it. Aggressive strategies soon lead to the destructive control of others.

> *"I didn't know there was any other way to handle it. When anyone came on me, I knew I could get them away by being the bully. I was pretty good at it. They maybe didn't respect me, but they sure feared me."*

It would be difficult to say there could never be a time in a person's life when aggressive action or violence would be useful. Some believe that violence and aggressive behaviors can act as a safety valve to lower tension. Research indicates that the reverse may be true—violence *nurtures* violence. Violent acts result in even greater violence. Violence and aggression tend to increase confusion in a conflict situation. It makes each side more rigid, increasing alienation and making meaningful communication impossible.

**Avoidance.** Running away or avoiding a conflict by withdrawing from the situation, ignoring the problem, or denying feelings are seldom useful solutions. When we choose to avoid, we choose to lose. Perhaps we may feel that the relationship is not worth maintaining, but more likely we choose to lose because we lack sufficient skills to negotiate a better resolution of the problem.

In effective conflict management, it is important to place these strategies in their proper perspectives by presenting a much wider choice of possible responses.

## Handling Conflicts Constructively

When handled constructively, conflicts are extremely valuable. We grow as a result of how we handle the adversities in our lives. By being aware of a variety of strategies that can be used to resolve conflicts, we can handle most conflicts with ease.

Conflicts can arise as a result of our relationships with other people. If there were no conflicts, our lives might become stagnant. While we may not actively seek conflicts, we can rise to the challenges when they occur. It would be folly to avoid doing anything that might cause conflict and frustration.

> *"When we decided to put on a musical, I never dreamed that we would have so many problems. Everyone wanted to be on the committees, but no one wanted to take the responsibilities of chairing them. It was a long six weeks, but what a great finale!"*

Educational Media Corporation®

It is possible to become set in our ways and to lose our effectiveness. We need to reexamine our needs, goals, and the procedures we are using to meet them. Conflicts revitalize our existing practices so adjustment can be made to new conditions.

Conflicts can also encourage personal and group change, reduce boredom, stimulate interest, spark curiosity, and provide avenues for bringing problems out into the open. Conflicts allow us to test and assess ourselves, to readjust the balance of power between individuals, and to increase our motivation and energy.

> *"I thought I knew what I wanted to accomplish when I was elected to student government. But, I changed my mind as we debated the issues. The others had a lot of great ideas and I got to know many of them better."*

Greater self-understanding and greater awareness of our values and identity can result from conflicts. Similar to the team cohesiveness that develops in sports contests, conflicts between groups can produce group cohesiveness.

Closely related to the growth that occurs as a result of conflict is the growth that occurs from taking risks.

## Taking Socially Acceptable Risks

Psychologists have long contended that it is important for us to take some risks to enrich our lives. It is helpful, however, to know the difference between socially acceptable risks and risks that are harmful to ourselves and others. Socially acceptable risk taking normally does not put us in conflict with others. Sometimes, however, we must negotiate such things as the time, the place, and the appropriateness of the behavior we wish to engage in to avoid conflicting with the needs and values of others.

> *"I thought no one would object to a presentation on 'safe sex practices.' Little did I realize that there is a large number of people who believe that the only safe sex practice is total abstinence. How are we going to educate those people who are already sexually active to practice 'safe sex' if we can't even talk about methods other than abstinence?"*

## Planned Stresses and Challenges

One excellent example of socially acceptable risk taking can be found in the popular area of outdoor and adventure education. Through a variety of activities, including ropes courses, adventure education provides an approach to physical activity which combines a joyful sense of adventure, a willingness to move beyond previously set limits, and the satisfaction of solving problems together.

In these programs young people voluntarily submit themselves to stressful situations. They are encouraged to "push the envelope" in situations which require dependence on both their inner strengths and upon others. The conflicts that arise in these situations, both internal and external, provide the fuel for the growth of the individuals and the group.

> *"I can't imagine that my folks paid money for me to come up here on this mountain to freeze. Every bone in my body aches. Would I do it again? Never. Am I glad I did it once? Yes!"*

## Summary

Conflicts are often approached with confusion. Conflict management should become a deliberate and intentional process in our lives—a well-developed skill rather than an area left to random emotional decisions.

Individuals who respond to conflicts with verbal and physical violence are often closed to other alternatives. Although avoiding confrontation can be useful at times, it can also lead to further insecurity and withdrawal.

Without conflicts, our lives would be very dull. Psychologists recommend that we take some socially accepted risks to enrich our lives. Planned stress challenge activities allow us to move beyond previously set limits and to experience the joy of cooperating with others to solve problems.

In chapter 6 we will look at some traditional advice for managing conflicts more effectively.

## Activities/Discussion

1. If we are going to change how we manage conflicts, we first must recognize the negative effects or costs of poorly managed conflicts. Identify a conflict that you had recently that you managed *badly*. What was the result? How might you have managed that conflict better?

2. Identify a conflict that you had recently that you managed *properly*. What strategy did you use in managing that conflict?

3. Avoiding a conflict can lead to insecurity and withdrawal. Under what type of circumstances have you chosen to flee or *avoid* a conflict? Is there a conflict in your life that you have been avoiding? What are some possible solutions to the situation?

4. Under what type of circumstances have you chosen to fight or to use *violence* in a conflict? Give an example of a time when you chose this method of reacting to a conflict.

5. Identify a situation in which you found yourself in conflict with someone that resulted in a growth experience for you. What did you learn from the experience?

6. What socially acceptable risks do you take to add spice to your life? What are you risking? Physical safety? Psychological safety? Financial security?

7. What fears would you have to overcome to participate in a stress challenge activity such as a ropes course?

8. Identify some risks that others take that might not be considered socially acceptable. What socially acceptable risks could you suggest as replacements for these activities?

# 6

# Traditional Strategies for Coping with Conflicts

*"When I was a boy of fourteen, my father was so ignorant I could hardly stand to have the old man around. But when I got to be twenty-one, I was astonished at how much he had learned in seven years."*

**Mark Twain**

Conflicts have been with us since the beginning of time. Everyone can expect to encounter conflicts frequently. Unfortunately, many of us lack the skills for dealing effectively with conflicts. We often are overwhelmed when we find ourselves in conflict. If we have not learned conflict management skills in advance of the crisis, we are likely to respond in an inappropriate manner under stress. We must be prepared to cope with conflicts when they arise.

There are ways to avoid conflicts and there are ways of dealing effectively with them when they do occur. Much can be gained by learning from the experiences and knowledge of others older and wiser than we are.

## Sayings and Proverbs

Knowledge can be found in sayings and proverbs for relating with one another and for resolving conflicts.

Which of the following reflect how you normally might react if you were to find yourself in conflict with someone?

*"Come and let us reason together."*

*"You scratch my back, I'll scratch yours."*

*"If you cannot make someone think as you do, make that person do as you think."*

*"A half a loaf is better than no loaf at all."*

*"A bird in the hand is better than two in the bush."*

*"The best way of handling conflicts is to avoid them."*

*"Avoid foolish and ignorant disputes, do not generate strife."*

*"Speak softly and carry a big stick."*

*"He who runs away lives to fight another day."*

*"Might overcomes right."*

*"Justice will prevail."*

*"Truth is mightier than the sword."*

*"Tit for tat is fair play."*

*"Kill your enemies with kindness."*

*"There is nothing so important that it is worth fighting for."*

Is there another proverb or saying that more typically describes how you would react?

## Possible Responses to Conflicts

Conflicts sometimes seem more complicated than they are. Some problems are difficult, if not impossible, to solve. However, many conflicts can be resolved by some easy-to-use strategies. Effective mediators help others to recall these strategies and to use them in resolving their conflicts. Continued application of these strategies will make the solution of future problems easier.

## 1. Become More Tolerant

Upon more careful reflection, some things are just not worth getting into a conflict over. You can defer to the wishes of another when the conflict is not worthy of your time or energy. You will not lose anything by choosing to avoid minor conflicts that really have no lasting significance. You are less threatened by deferring to others when you have positive feelings about yourself.

One of your English teachers always wants papers folded in a certain way. You could rebel, or you could decide that it is not important to you how the papers are folded, so you do it the teacher's way. Remember, some issues are not worth the energy it takes to raise them.

## 2. Let Chance Decide

All of the alternatives available are about equal in terms of their advantages and disadvantages for both of you. A flip of the coin can resolve the issue between relatively equal alternatives. The "luck of the draw" decides the situation.

Pizza or hamburgers tonight? You and your date like them both, so why not just flip a coin? Heads it's pizza, tails it's hamburgers.

## 3. Share—Take Turns

There are some things that are too expensive for everyone to own. Other things are not in use all the time. By pooling our resources, we can have access to things that we could not afford by ourselves. However, sometimes two of us want to use the same thing at the same time. The result is a conflict. One way of resolving a conflict when resources are limited is to share—take turns. "You use the computer before supper and I'll use it this evening." Simple?

## 4. Compromise

You would like to go someplace special on Friday night. You were getting tired of pizza and a movie. You suggest burgers and bowling, but your boyfriend likes the familiar routine; he's not very good at bowling.

So, compromise! He gives up the pizza and you give up the bowling, and you have a change. Not a big change, granted, but you have introduced variety in your routine through compromise.

## 5. Offer Your Apology

When a conflict is a clash between different values and ideas, it causes unpleasant feelings in the other person. If, upon reflection, you determine that your position was too strong or that you were in error, you might apologize. A sincere "I'm sorry" communicates that you have some feeling—some empathy—for the other person and that you regret any discomfort caused.

## 6. Recognize the Validity of the Other's Position

After you have heard the other person's point of view on the issue, you might simply choose to acknowledge that person's ideas and/or feelings as having sufficient merit to win you over. As we learn to listen to and respect the feelings of others, we often learn that people's feelings are more important than things. There are things in life more important than getting our way or winning our point.

## 7. Postpone the Decision

The relationship has been getting serious. She wants to get married as soon as graduation is over. You are not sure you are ready to settle down. The talk about a wedding intensifies and you are becoming confused as to how you really feel about her. You are not sufficiently in control of your feelings and your situation to want to make a decision about marriage. You both decide to postpone any further talk or plans about marriage until you both can deal with the issue equally.

## 8. Interject Humor

Do you take yourself too seriously? Are you capable of laughing with others, not at them? Often a situation requires some type of tension relief. If both of you can laugh at the ridiculousness of the dilemma, sometimes the tension can be reduced and the conflict defused.

## 9. Look for a Fresh Approach

When nothing seems to work and the conflict still rages, it is time to open your options by radically departing from tradition and look for a new approach to the situation. The services of a mediator are particularly useful in helping people in conflict to seek those alternatives, evaluate the consequences of each alternative, and to put a new plan into action.

## Summary

There are many traditional ways of responding to conflicts. Becoming more tolerant of others will reduce conflicts. When the alternatives are nearly equal, let chance decide. Taking turns and compromising may also be acceptable solutions.

If you discover you were in error, your apology might end the conflict. After listening to the other person, you could choose to allow the other's point of view to dominate. Humor sometimes diffuses a conflict when both can laugh at the ridiculousness of the situation.

When a solution does not seem possible at the time, postponing the decision will allow time for more information-gathering and for feelings to change.

When traditional approaches fail, look for a fresh approach, perhaps engaging the services of a mediator. How you define the conflict or problem determines how you will approach solving it. We will look at the process of defining conflicts in chapter 7.

## Activities/Discussion

1. Look back on a conflict that seemed serious at the time. Can you see humor in the situation now? How might you have interjected some humor at the time?

2. When might it not be a good time to postpone a decision? What type of conflicts benefit by delaying decisions?

3. Is there someone to whom you owe an apology for a position you have taken that has kept a conflict alive? How and when might you offer that apology?

4. Can you identify a time when you compromised to resolve a conflict? Was the result acceptable to both parties?

5. List some conflicts that you have had in the past that could have been resolved had you decided at the time that the issue was not worth the energy.

# 7

# Defining the Conflict

*"We really didn't know what the problem was until we started to talk about it. Talking about it helped us to see what we needed to do to solve it."*

Conflict resolution skills can be taught and young people are eager to learn techniques that will help them cope more effectively with life's situations.

How you describe or define a conflict or problem affects how you will attempt to resolve it. For successful conflict resolution, it is important to develop a skill for defining conflicts. There are several important steps to defining conflicts in ways that aid in their resolution. These steps are as follows:

## 1. Describe the conflict in a win/win rather than a win/lose or lose/win fashion.

Both sides have something invested in the problem and its solution. You must see the conflict as something that can be solved by working together for a mutually satisfying solution.

*"I get so angry when he takes over. He makes so many more mistakes than I do. I hope the boss can see how he is botching the job."*

**Win/lose.** If you perceive your situation as a *win/lose* relationship, nothing good will result. It will be difficult to ever establish a cooperative relationship with this person because of the way you perceive the basic relationship. You may build yourself up, but the other person will feel resentful and try to cut off communication. Defining the conflict in a win/lose manner promotes distrust, dislike, deception, rivalry, and threats. Your relationship will continue to deteriorate as long as you perceive it in this fashion.

*"I don't care any more. You can do whatever you want. You'd do it your way anyway, so why do you bother to ask me?"*

**Lose/win.** If you perceive the situation as a *lose/win* relationship, you are saying that you do not care enough about the relationship or that you lack the skills to resolve the conflict.

**Win/win.** Define the conflict as a *mutual* problem to be solved. This will increase communication, trust, and respect for each other. No one loses when two people sit down to solve a mutual problem.

> *"Martha and I are having difficulty deciding who should do the dishes on Friday night. We both have other things we would rather do."*

When everything you do reflects your belief that the conflict should be seen as a *win/win* proposition, you also are modeling the position you desire the other person to take.

## 2. Don't label or judge the other person in the conflict.

When you describe the person with whom you have a conflict, do *not* label or judge that person's actions.

> *"He pretends he is better than I am, but he is so stupid!"*

Labeling creates mistrust, misunderstanding, and resentment. Do not label, accuse, or insult the other person. It is difficult to respond to a label in a constructive manner. Instead, describe what the other person has done to provoke the conflict.

By avoiding the use of labels, the other person will become aware that you also wish to be described in terms of your behavior and not to be accused or insulted.

## 3. Be *specific* about the actions of the other person in the conflict.

Don't make the conflict into a catastrophe; confine your definition of the conflict to the specific behavior that is upsetting you. Don't generalize. Be specific.

> *"She criticizes me all the time. I can't do anything to please her" (too general).*
>
> *"Yesterday I brought up the fact that we had to get the report done by Friday. She walked away without saying anything" (more specific).*

Any generalizations made by the other person should be challenged until that person identifies the specific behavior of yours that is perceived to be contributing to the conflict.

Educational Media Corporation®

## 4. Describe how the other person's behavior makes you feel, and what you are considering doing as a result of your feelings.

When you give feedback to another person about something that irritates you, make sure it is something worthy of attention. Then, be specific about the behavior, tell how the other person's behavior affects you, and tell what you are considering doing. Do not tell the other person what to do.

*"When you move my homework from the table without my permission, it makes me very angry. I'm not sure I want to bring it home anymore."*

Understanding *your* feelings and intentions are as important as understanding the other person. You must first be able to identify your feelings before you can share them with others. The person with whom you are in conflict cannot be a mind reader.

There is a tendency in conflicts to hide feelings and reactions from each other. You often do not want others to know how upset you really are. If conflicts are to be resolved, you need to share your feelings and reactions. This helps others to understand how their actions are affecting you. Perhaps they will reciprocate by sharing how your behavior is affecting them.

## 5. Describe what you could do to change your reaction to the situation.

The only person you can control or change is you. If you find yourself in conflict with another, what choices do you have to resolve the conflict?

*"I guess I could do my homework in my room. Then it wouldn't be in your way when you are setting the table for supper."*

If you wish to resolve a conflict, you must begin by deciding how *you* can change *your* actions. It would be nice if everyone else changed so you would never have to. But you do not have control over the actions of others; they do. You can only control your own actions. You can change your actions much more easily than you can change another person's behavior.

Neglecting to do something constructive helps to create and continue the conflict just as much as doing something destructive. Knowing how your actions affect the conflict is essential for planning how to resolve it.

## Summary

The five steps for defining a conflict are very important for facilitating the resolution of the problem.

1. Define the conflict as a mutual problem to be solved, not as a win-lose struggle.

2. Describe the other person's actions; don't label, accuse, or insult. Make sure the conflict is over issues and actions, not personalities.

3. Define the conflict in the smallest and most specific way possible.

4. Describe your feelings about and your reactions to the other person's actions.

5. Define your actions (what are you doing and neglecting to do) to help create and continue the conflict.

Constructive management of a conflict begins with *your* actions, *your* feelings, *your* skills and assets, *your* willingness to change, and *your* ability to define the conflict in a helpful way.

An analysis of how *not* to resolve a conflict provided some guidelines in chapter 8 for facilitating conflict resolution.

## Activities/Discussion

1. Identify an area of conflict that currently exists between you and another person. Be sure and define the conflict as a win/win situation.

2. Describe the other person. Avoid labeling and judging that individual.

3. List the specific behaviors of the other person that are contributing to the conflict.

4. Write a statement about how those behaviors are affecting you. Identify your feelings and what you are considering doing as a result of those feelings.

5. What are you doing, or neglecting to do, to keep the conflict going?

6. What can you do to bring the conflict to an end?

# 8

# A Bill of Rights for Individuals in Conflict

*"Don't people have anything better to do than to air their dirty linen in public? Is anything really resolved when so many people get involved?"*

During 1991 a conflict between two individuals focused the nation's attention to the issue of sexual harassment. Professor Anita Hill's accusation that her former employer, Clarence Thomas, sexually harassed her several years previously severely complicated the confirmation process for Supreme

Court-nominee, Thomas. As we watched the conflict unfold in the public hearings, some ideas of how *not* to resolve conflicts emerged.

From this very public experience of two people in conflict, it is suggested that there needs to be a "bill of rights" for those who find themselves in conflict with one another. Respecting these rights would greatly aid in the resolution of any conflict.

Suggestions for this "bill of rights" follow:

## 1. The right to timeliness.

Anita Hill waited several years before making her conflict with Thomas known. Many viewers believed that even if Thomas were guilty, it was inappropriate for Hill to wait several years before bringing the conflict out into the open. Cooperative resolution of the conflict is easier if the issue is dealt with shortly after it occurs.

## 2. The right to direct confrontation.

Anita Hill never confronted her accuser directly. Hill never gave Thomas the opportunity to resolve the differences between them in private. Many speculated as to the purity of Anita Hill's motives to make things right when she went public with the conflict rather than confront her offender personally.

## 3. The right to privacy.

Resolution of conflict is best done in private. When one or more party refuses to negotiate in good faith, many times the conflict is "leaked" to others. Public attention to the conflict changes the nature of the conflict and makes resolution of the original conflict more difficult.

## 4. The right to an egalitarian relationship.

When the parties in the conflict do not perceive themselves as equals, it is difficult to approach the other person in the conflict. Anita Hill claimed Thomas' role as her employer intimidated her. She said it kept her from confronting him about his behavior at the time. She delayed dealing with the conflict because she believed that she was in a no win (lose/win) situation as his employee. Conflict resolution requires that we be in a position to see the problem as a mutual one that *equals* can solve in a win/win situation.

Here are some rules for establishing an egalitarian partnership which is essential in conflict resolution:

- Each person gets a turn to speak.
- There are no interruptions.
- Each person must agree not to make negative comments about the other.
- Each person must listen to the other.
- Each person must agree to consider things from the other's perspective rather than focusing only on one's own thoughts.

## 5. The right to consent or dissent.

Both individuals involved should have the right to terminate the relationship with the other person or to build upon the relationship, using the knowledge obtained by cooperating to resolve the conflict. How much liberty do we have in approaching or avoiding the territory of another? How do we obtain the consent of another to participate in conflict resolution?

## 6. The right to change and grow.

If we accept the fact that people can and do change, and that they can and do grow from their past mistakes, how appropriate is it to bring up old offenses and past short-comings? Closely related to the right to timeliness, it is important that the discussion center on the current conflict and not on the past.

## 7. The right to apologize or correct the situation.

If the other person is the offender, direct confrontation provides an opportunity for that person to apologize or to offer to make the situation right. When we deny direct confrontation, we make it difficult for anyone to apologize or to make amends.

## 8. The right to forgive and to receive forgiveness.

It has often been said that what we need is more love in the world. Love bridges many gaps caused by conflicts. People who know how to love also know how to forgive and to accept the forgiveness of others. In a conflict, the *offended* person has the opportunity to end the conflict by forgiving the other. Rather than harboring a sense of guilt, the *offending* person has the *choice* to accept the forgiveness and to put the conflict to rest. Forgiveness is a powerful tool for restoring relationships between individuals in conflict. "To every thing there is a season... a time to love, and a time to hate... a time of war, and a time of peace. (Ecclesiastes 3: 1, 8).

# Summary

Conflict resolution can best be done in private with the people in conflict confronting each other directly. This confrontation should occur in a timely fashion. The conflict should be defined as a win/win proposition with both individuals having equal status in the resolution process.

Participation in the process should be voluntary. Each person in the dispute has a right to consent or dissent concerning any attempts to resolve the problem. The conflict should be confined to the specific issue at hand.

Attempts to broaden the conflict to include past transgressions should be resisted. People can and do change, growing from their past mistakes. Apologies and offers to change should be accepted, when appropriate, and the offended persons should be willing to put the conflict to rest at the appropriate time.

These "rights" will be taken into consideration as we present a model for mediation in Part II.

## Activities/Discussion

1. Which of the "bill of rights" listed previously would be the most important to you if you were to find yourself in a conflict with someone?

2. What keeps some people from putting a conflict behind them, even when the other person offers an apology?

3. How would you establish an egalitarian relationship between two people in conflict if one of the persons is a teacher and the other is a student?

4. What is gained by bringing a conflict between two people into public view? What steps should be taken before such action is taken?

# Part II

# Mediation

# 9

# An Introduction to Mediation

*"I tried to talk with her, but she wouldn't listen. She just got mad and hung up. I asked a friend if he would try to reason with her. He didn't want to get involved, but he suggested that I contact the peer mediation service."*

Mediation is the process of intervening in the lives of others to help them resolve conflicts. Mediation provides an opportunity for persons who are in conflict to listen to, to understand, and to respect the views of others. Communication between the disputing persons is improved and cooperation is sought for solving a common problem. The conflict is defined as a win/win situation and a mutually satisfying solution is agreed upon and implemented.

Although conflicts can involve more than two people, for the sake of clarity, we will discuss the process of mediating disputes between two individuals.

---

## The Role of the Mediator

Mediation can be a quick and fair way to resolve a conflict if the persons involved agree to the participation of a mediator. While it is sometimes advisable to use more than one mediator, for the purpose of clarity, we will refer to the mediator in the singular. Mediators are neutral third persons who are trained to lead mediation sessions. They do not take sides; they serve as impartial listeners and facilitators to help those involved come to an agreement. Mediators re-direct the energy of others from being adversaries to becoming partners, cooperating in the solution of a mutual problem.

Peer mediators are caring persons who have been trained as peer helpers. They have supplemented their training in communication and helping skills with strategies for conflict resolution and mediation.

The same rules of confidentiality apply to peer mediation that apply to other peer helping projects. The things that are shared in the mediation session are private—privileged communication—and they are not to be shared with anyone.

## Mediation Defined

*Webster* defined mediation as: friendly or diplomatic intervention, usually by consent or invitation, for settling differences between persons, nations, and so forth.

1. **Intervention.** Intervention is coming between individuals to help settle a dispute. Even though it is well-intended, an intervention is involvement in the lives of others.

2. **Friendly or diplomatic..., usually by consent or invitation.** These terms provide the important qualifiers for getting involved in the lives of others. Generally, peer helpers should confine their interventions to times when they are invited. The participants should consent to being a part of the mediation process. If consent is not obtained, the peer helper intercedes only to define and offer the services available, inviting them to participate in the mediation process. When the mediator utilizes the communication skills provided in most peer helper training programs, the helper has a good chance of being perceived by the participants as friendly and diplomatic.

3. **For settling differences.** Mediation deals with helping others solve conflicts and to resolve problems. The mediators must be well trained in systematic procedures for conflict resolution. Upon the conclusion of mediation, all parties should understand the process of conflict resolution so they can apply this process themselves to future conflicts.

4. **Between persons, nations, and so forth.** Conflict resolution strategies can be applied to disputes between individuals, groups, and even nations. A more peaceful world will result from an understanding and application of an effective conflict resolution model on all levels.

Educational Media Corporation®

## Conditions for Participation

Mediation is based on the assumption that the participants are mutually agreeable to having a neutral third person help them resolve their conflict. Before beginning mediation, the participants also should agree to:

- Commit the necessary time for the session.
- Meet in the agreed upon time and place.
- Acknowledge the responsibility and the authority of the mediator to preside over the session.
- Share their own wants, needs, feelings, and perceptions of the conflict.
- Listen to the other person's point of view without interrupting.
- Avoid labeling, judging, or blaming the other person.
- Remain calm and control their anger.
- Define the conflict as a win/win proposition.
- Brainstorm possible solutions without evaluating them prematurely.
- Commit to a solution that is agreeable to both.

A printed form similar to the one on pages 108-109 can be utilized listing these conditions. You can review each of the items with the participants to obtain their verbal agreement. The success of mediation depends on laying a good foundation for cooperation.

## Guidelines for Supervision

Peer mediation should always be a project—an extension—of an organized peer helping program. Your authority as a peer mediator is delegated to you by your trainer and supervisor. As the supervising adult, that person is responsible for your actions while you are functioning in your assigned role. It is extremely important that you keep your supervisor informed of your progress—your successes and your failures. Regular supervisory sessions should be held where you can exchange ideas and feelings.

## Making Appropriate Referrals

Your peer helper training has been designed to provide the basic communication and helping skills necessary for you to participate successfully in a variety of projects. You will be able to experience success in most situations by carefully following the guidelines in your training. However, when you encounter situations that extend beyond your training, make an immediate referral to your supervisor. You are not expected to be able to successfully mediate every situation. As a peer helper, you are expected to help individuals obtain appropriate assistance.

## Summary

Mediation is friendly or diplomatic intervention, usually by consent or invitation, for settling differences between persons. It is a process for helping others to define their conflicts as win/win situations. Mediators are neutral persons trained to serve as impartial listeners to help people involved in conflicts come to agreements. Peer mediators are skilled peer helpers with additional training in conflict resolution and mediation.

Participants in mediation agree to having a neutral third person help them resolve their conflicts. Peer mediators should maintain close contact with their supervisors to share successes, failures, and to make referrals.

Mediation is an orderly process that begins with a campaign to inform potential users of the nature and availability of the program. In chapter 10 we will detail fifteen essentials steps for effective mediation.

## Activities/Discussion

1. Have you ever asked someone to help you to resolve a conflict with another person? How did you choose that person?

2. What personal characteristics would you expect a mediator to possess? You might want to review the helping characteristics presented in your peer helper training program. Can these characteristics be learned?

3. Can you force someone to participate in a mediation session? How might you proceed to inform someone of the availability of mediation services?

4. Under what conditions would you be unable to keep what is said in a mediation session confidential? You might want to review the guidelines concerning confidentiality that were a part of your peer helper training.

5. Explain the process you would use in making a referral. What would be one sign that a person required more assistance than you were prepared to offer?

Educational Media Corporation®

# 10

# A 15-Step Peer Mediation Program

*"I saw the notice on the bulletin board about peer mediation. I didn't pay much attention. Now I've got this problem with Ted. Maybe I should check into this mediation stuff a little more."*

The process of mediation should be orderly. Each step builds on the successful completion of the earlier steps. Here are fifteen steps that should be given attention in a viable peer mediation program.

## The peer mediator should:

1. Inform others that a mediation service exists.

2. Obtain consent from those involved in the conflict to become involved in mediation.

3. Secure a safe and private location for the sharing of information.

4. Explain the need to be a good listener as the other speaks.

5. Encourage each person to tell what happened while the other listens.

6. Have each person summarize what the other person said.

7. Help both individuals identify their feelings.

8. Summarize the two positions, emphasizing the points of agreement as well as the points of contention.

9. Seek agreement from both people with the summary.

10. Ask each person to offer suggestions on how the conflict can be resolved.

11. Help the participants evaluate the choices.

12. Seek agreement for a tentative settlement.

13. Obtain a written commitment from both persons to implement the chosen solution.

14. Make arrangements to follow up this mediation session to see how the agreement is working.

15. At the request of either person, repeat the process if any person fails to live up to the agreement.

Let us look at each of these steps in detail:

## 1. The peer mediator should inform others that a mediation service exists.

Any good program providing assistance to others must have good public relations. People need to know that a service is available before they actually need to use it. Newspaper articles about the mediation program, public address announcements, and posters are some ways to announce your mediation service.

Students can be educated as to the process of mediation by the use of role plays or skits. A demonstration of how a mediator would work with two people to resolve a conflict could be presented during home room periods.

Once a demonstration has been performed successfully, it can be videotaped and replayed to orient others to the process of mediation. Peer helpers can lead a discussion on conflict resolution and mediation following the viewing of the videotape.

Consider presenting programs about your mediation service to community groups. Radio, cable television, and local television stations also provide opportunities for you to share information about your program with the community.

Since there is a certain element of crisis in most conflicts, the services of a mediator should be available with a minimum of delay. Peer helpers serving as mediators can be "on call" during a specific period of the day. Contacting the mediator is usually done through a central location such as the guidance office.

## 2. The peer mediator should obtain consent from those involved in the conflict to become involved in mediation.

When two people are in conflict, often it is a concerned third party that first sees the need for mediation. This person should propose the possibility of mediation and aid the individuals in conflict to make the appropriate contact. Participation in mediation should be voluntary.

If any of those involved in the conflict do not consent to participate in mediation, the mediator or another qualified third party should provide a more detailed explanation of the process of mediation. Others can share concern for the individuals involved, but the choice whether or not to participate in mediation belongs to the persons in conflict.

Submitting a conflict to mediation also requires that the participants be *committed* to the process. A commitment is a promise we make to ourselves and others that we keep no matter what. It's not based on circumstances; it does not depend on the actions of others. A commitment is rooted within each person and is entirely dependent upon one's willingness to generate it.

Ask each person, "Are *you* willing to be committed to working out your differences?" Let both people know that sometimes they have to take the first step themselves to resolve a conflict.

## 3. The peer mediator should secure a safe and private location for the sharing of information.

Conflict mediation requires the undivided attention of the individuals involved. An audience is not desired. Always respect the rights for privacy for all persons. Take the time to defuse the situation by removing the discussion about the conflict from the eyes and ears of those who are not directly involved.

If a counseling office or conference room is not available, select an empty classroom or any location that offers separation from others. Remind the participants that mediation works only when everyone involved respects the rights of others to share their opinions and feelings in confidence.

## 4. The peer mediator should explain the need to be a good listener as others speak.

Conflicts cannot be resolved unless all of the necessary information is "placed on the table." This requires good listening. Labeling or judging another tends to cause that person to "shut down" and not share important information.

Educational Media Corporation®

## 5. The peer mediator should encourage each person to tell what happened while the other listens.

Both individuals will have equal opportunity to talk and to explain the situation as they perceive it. Listeners need to be reminded that they will be asked to summarize what the other person said.

Ask open questions to obtain additional information so you fully understand each person's position.

## 6. The peer mediator should have each person summarize what the other person said.

While it is hard not to be thinking about what you will say when your turn comes, if you know you will be asked to summarize what you have heard, it is necessary for you to listen to what is being said. Don't overload the listener with too much information. Ask for a summary at appropriate intervals. Listeners may take notes to aid in the summary process.

## 7. The peer mediator should help both people identify their feelings.

It is important to be aware of feelings and their interrelationship with behaviors. We behave in response to our feelings and we feel in response to our behaviors and the behaviors of others. To change behavior, we need to be aware of feelings. Take time to uncover the feelings underlying the behaviors of both individuals. Identify whether they are experiencing pleasant feelings, unpleasant feelings, or both. Describe the feelings you are hearing with words from the lists on page 36.

## 8. The peer mediator should summarize the two positions, emphasizing the points of agreement as well as the points of contention.

You have heard both sides. Now it is your turn to do what you can to further clarify the situation. Clearly outline points of agreement as well as points of disagreement. It helps to see that there are many areas of agreement, and to see clearly the points for which disagreement remains.

## 9. The peer mediator should seek agreement from both individuals with the summary.

Do both individuals agree with your summary? Have you made any errors? Has anything been overlooked? If not, you have made considerable progress just getting agreement on what the disagreement is.

## 10. The peer mediator should ask each person to offer suggestions on how the conflict can be resolved.

Every conflict has solutions. However, the solutions might not be the most acceptable alternative for one or more of the people involved. Solving conflicts requires that we are willing to integrate our needs to find a solution. Begin by listing possible solutions, without evaluating their possible consequences. We often call this process "brainstorming." You do not have to list every possible alternative, but you do have to list several options—however ridiculous or impractical they may seem—to generate a viable solution. Avoid offering alternatives of your own until the others have exhausted all of their possibilities.

## 11. The peer mediator should help the participants evaluate the choices.

Review the list of alternatives generated by the brainstorming session. Some alternatives can be dismissed immediately by mutual agreement without further discussion. The remaining alternatives should be explored in greater depth. List the positive consequences and the negative consequences to each alternative seriously considered.

## 12. The peer mediator should seek agreement for a tentative settlement.

With the alternatives and their consequences clearly before them, work toward an integrated solution. Sometimes the information obtained from the negotiations makes the appropriate solution obvious to all. Sometimes some compromising—sacrificing something to gain the greater goal of resolving the conflict—is necessary. Do not be in a hurry to end the discussion. Remember, conflicts can have positive benefits and can stimulate creative thinking.

If there is more than one issue to be resolved, seek tentative approval on what you perceive to be the issue with the least conflict. However, keep all of the issues on the table. In order to resolve the entire conflict, it might be necessary to re-negotiate the tentative solution to the first issue.

If no tentative settlement is agreed upon, return to brainstorming and generate more positive alternatives. Be careful not to judge the merits of the alternatives until the brainstorming session ends. Prematurely judging and evaluating alternatives can stifle the creative process.

Educational Media Corporation®

## 13. The peer mediator should obtain a written commitment from both people to implement the chosen solution.

A great deal of energy has been invested in this process up to this point. It is advisable to seal the agreement by setting the terms of the settlement in writing. Encourage them to write a contract, however brief. A written contract often is perceived as being more binding that a verbal agreement. Write down any decisions or agreements—ones that are based upon full discussion and participation.

As the session proceeds, you may wish to thank each person who expresses an opinion or idea. This acknowledges participation and encourages those who might tend to be reluctant to get more involved.

## 14. The peer mediator should make arrangements to follow up this mediation session to see how the agreement is working.

To adequately evaluate your success as a mediator, and the success of the mediation program, it is important that you follow up each intervention to see if the resolution agreed upon remains in effect for a specified period of time. You can talk to each participant individually, or you can arrange for them to meet together if further mediation is required.

Questionnaires can be sent to persons who participated in mediation to obtain feedback concerning how they perceived the service.

## 15. The peer mediator should, at the request of either person, repeat the process if any person fails to live up to the agreement.

It is not your purpose to provide an on-going relationship with the people that were involved in the mediation. However, success can be claimed only if the conflict remains resolved. The mediation process should be repeated, if necessary, if the conflict continues. Before you end the mediation session, inform both individuals that they should feel free to contact you if either person fails to live up to the agreement. A successful resolution of the conflict should produce some advocates for your mediation program.

## Summary

Laying a good foundation is important to the success of your peer mediation program. Publicity can inform potential participants of the availability and the requirements of your peer mediation program. Participants must give their consent to participate and to cooperate prior to beginning mediation. In privacy, the participants state their positions, share their feelings, and search for a win/win solution to the conflict. A written commitment from both persons to implement the agreed upon solution increases the chances that the process will be successful.

In chapter 11 we will provide an overview of the peer mediation process.

## Discussion Questions

1. What opportunities exist in your school for publicizing your peer mediation program? Remember to inform students, faculty, and administration about the services and how people can take advantage of it.

2. How can you get someone to participate in peer mediation if that person initially rejects the service?

3. What should you do if none of the alternatives suggested during mediation are acceptable to both?

# 11

# An Overview of the Peer Mediation Process

*"I knew I shouldn't have done it. He asked me if he could borrow my biology notes. I not only lost my notes, I lost my friend. I am so angry."*

Now it is time to put it all together. You have reviewed the nature of conflicts and explored the mediation process. You have two people coming in for mediation in a few moments and you are looking for a model—an outline.

## Preparation

Arrive at the agreed upon place before the scheduled time for the session to begin. In selecting a location, remember privacy is essential to insure confidentiality.

Before the others arrive, there are a few things you can do to prepare. A table with three chairs makes for a very business-like setting. Care should be taken to arrange the furniture so all participants can see each other without difficulty. You also will want pens and blank copies of any forms you will use.

## Welcome

Welcome both participants and thank them for coming. If you have not met before, introduce yourself and ask them to say their names. Decide how you will address each other. It is not necessary to be too formal. However, if one of the persons involved in the conflict being mediated is a teacher, administrator, or parent, you might choose to treat everyone equally by addressing them formally, i.e. Mr. Smith, Ms. Sanchez.

## Orientation

Review some of the key concepts about mediation with your participants. Remember, this may be their first exposure to mediation. Laying a good foundation is essential to success.

*"Conflicts can be solved if we agree to work together to find a solution. Mediation provides a quick and fair way to resolving conflicts.*

*Today I am going to serve as your mediator. I have been trained to lead mediation sessions like this one.*

*I will not take sides. I will listen to what each of you have to say and help you to state your positions clearly. It is important that each of you share your needs, feelings, and perceptions of the situation that has caused this conflict. I will restate what I hear each of you saying. I also will ask each of you to restate the position of the other person.*

*It is important that both of you agree to certain things before we begin. Arriving at a mutually agreeable solution is much easier if you agree to some basic procedures. Here is a list of the items that I would like you to agree to before we begin.*

*You both have a lot of energy that has resulted from this conflict. It is my hope that we will be able to re-direct that energy that has made you adversaries so that you can become partners in solving this problem.*

*Sometimes when a disagreement arises between people, we believe that the only solution is that one person will win and the other will lose. Today I am asking you to look at the problem as one that has a win/win solution. If we put all of our creative energy to work, I am confident that we can come up with a solution that will be better than any solution where one of you wins and the other loses.*

*Are you willing to give it a try?*

*Good! Let's look at the list of ground rules."*

---

# Ground Rules for Mediation

Date _____

I, _____, have a conflict with

_____ over the issue of

_____.

I am interested in resolving this conflict through mediation.

**I agree to the following:**

❏ 1. I agree to spend the necessary time to meet with the person named above and a mediator.

❏ 2. I agree to meet:

Day/date: _____

Time: _____

Place: _____

❏ 3. I agree to respect the leadership of the mediator assigned and to follow the guidance and direction offered during the session.

❏ 4. I agree to share my side of the story. I will share my wants, needs, feelings, and perceptions of the conflict.

❏ 5. I agree to listen to the other person's point of view without interrupting.

Educational Media Corporation®

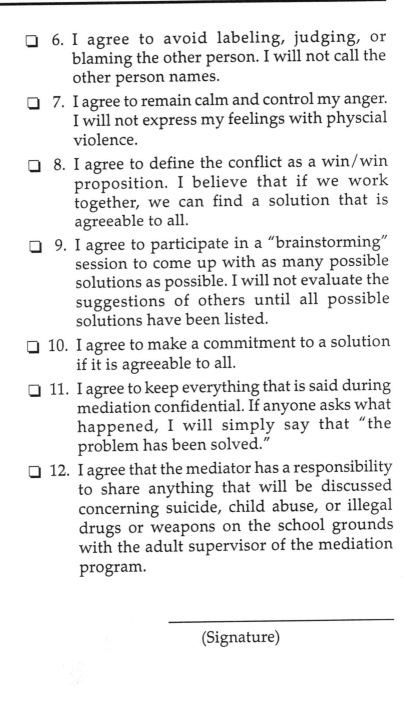

❏ 6. I agree to avoid labeling, judging, or blaming the other person. I will not call the other person names.

❏ 7. I agree to remain calm and control my anger. I will not express my feelings with physcial violence.

❏ 8. I agree to define the conflict as a win/win proposition. I believe that if we work together, we can find a solution that is agreeable to all.

❏ 9. I agree to participate in a "brainstorming" session to come up with as many possible solutions as possible. I will not evaluate the suggestions of others until all possible solutions have been listed.

❏ 10. I agree to make a commitment to a solution if it is agreeable to all.

❏ 11. I agree to keep everything that is said during mediation confidential. If anyone asks what happened, I will simply say that "the problem has been solved."

❏ 12. I agree that the mediator has a responsibility to share anything that will be discussed concerning suicide, child abuse, or illegal drugs or weapons on the school grounds with the adult supervisor of the mediation program.

_____

(Signature)

## Gathering Information

Someone has to begin. Decide which person should share first. Remind them that they have agreed not to interrupt. If the situation is tense and the individuals are uncomfortable with each other, ask them to speak to you, not to each other.

> *"Mike, would you please go first. Tell me what happened between you and Juan. Juan, I'd like you to listen to what Mike has to say without interrupting. Go ahead, Mike."*

At an appropriate break in Mike's sharing, summarize what you have heard.

> *"You loaned Juan your notes for biology so he could prepare for a test on Friday. He promised to give them back to you after the test so you would have them to study for your mid-term exam next week. Now he can't find his back pack and your notes were in it."*

Unless Mike's feelings about the situation were obvious to you from what he said, ask Mike to explore his feelings. Clarify his feelings by identifying whether the feelings you are hearing are pleasant, unpleasant, or both.

> *"You are very **upset** about not getting your biology notes back. You feel **sorry** for Juan— he lost his back pack and everything in it—but you are **irritated** with him for not taking better care of something that was so important to you."*

Ask the other person to describe his perceptions of what happened to cause the conflict. Summarize what you hear, highlight points of agreement as well as disagreement.

> *"Juan, you agree that you told Mike you would return his biology notes after his test. However, you don't believe that there is anything that you can do about the notes now that they are lost. You are **sorry** that this has happened and you are **disappointed** that Mike is blaming you because your back pack has disappeared. You are pretty sure you left your back pack on the bus. You called the bus company; they said it wasn't turned in."*

If you need additional information about the situation before attempting to generate possible solutions, ask some questions. Remember that high facilitative questions are *open* questions—questions that cannot be answered by yes, no, or a short response. High facilitative questions generally begin with who, what, when, where, or how, and *not* why.

> *"Juan, what steps have you taken to try and find your back pack? Where are some places that you might have left it?"*

> *"Mike, if Juan is unable to find his back pack and your notes, how might the lost notes be replaced?"*

You have clarified both positions, demonstrated that you understand the feelings shared by both individuals, and sought additional information by asking open questions.

## Confirming the Positions

Check with both individuals to see if they understood what the other said. Ask each person to restate what they heard the other person say.

> *"Juan, what have you heard Mike say about the situation? How does he feel? What does Mike want you to do?"*

> *"Mike, what did you hear Juan say? How does he feel? What does Juan expect from you?"*

## Generating Options

Often the best place to look for the solution to a conflict is within ourselves. Ask the participants what they each might do to resolve the conflict.

> *"Mike, what could you do that will change this situation and end the conflict? Don't tell Juan what he should do; look inside yourself to see if there is something you might do."*

There may be some resistance to take any responsibility for resolving the conflict. Remember, we always have a choice as to how we will react to any given situation. While we may not choose to act on our options, we do have choices.

> *"So, Mike, you could ask one of your friends for his notes.... oh, okay, **her** notes. You could get a photo copy of them so you'd have them to study. I realize they are not the same as your own notes, but they would be better than nothing."*

> *"Juan, what could you do to make this situation better?"*

One of the participants has demonstrated that he is willing to make some effort to change the situation. This can serve as a model for generating additional options.

*"You haven't given up looking for your back pack. Although you called the bus company, you said you could go down there and check their lost and found yourself."*

Although you cannot look at all the alternatives, you can utilize the creative energies of all present to generate some additional options.

*"You've come up with a couple of things that you each might do to resolve or lessen this conflict between you. What are some other possibilities? Let's just list them without discussing them. We'll decide which suggestions are practical later."*

## Resolving

After the brainstorming session, decide which options deserve further exploration. Be careful not to eliminate suggestions too easily. Further discussion of the alternatives and their consequences may lead to the most fruitful solution.

*"Juan, as we were talking it appears that there are other places you might look for your back pack. When Mike reminded you that you had swim team practice on Friday, you seemed to think there was a possibility that you left your back pack in the locker room. Would it be okay if we took a short break while you checked that possibility?"*

---

Mediators should remain flexible while working to resolve a conflict. If it appears that some immediate action is required to check out a viable option, an intermission is appropriate. Sometimes you may wish to break to discuss options with each person privately. If you have access to information that one person finds difficult to share in front of the other, you can be more effective in mediating a solution.

*"That's great, Juan. I am glad you found your back pack. Mike, now that you have your notes back, I guess this conflict has been resolved. However, I wonder what each of you has learned from this situation. What will each of you do differently in the future to keep something like this from happening again?"*

People who participate in mediation should do more than simply resolve the current conflict. Use this opportunity to help them understand what they can do to avoid similar conflicts in the future.

*"Mike, you have decided that it is not wise to loan something as valuable as your biology notes. In the future, how will you handle a request like you got from Juan so you do not lose his friendship?"*

Being more aware of the consequences of lost notes, Mike is willing to be more assertive in handling requests. A discussion of appropriate ways to respond to a similar request should be followed by asking Juan what he can do to avoid a similar conflict in the future.

*"Juan, you have decided that it isn't worth the risk to borrow something as valuable as someone's class notes. If you miss class in the future, you are going to talk with the instructor first and see if there is a handout. If that doesn't work, you are going to copy the notes and return them immediately."*

## Closing

As the session comes to a close, remind them to respect the rule of confidentiality concerning the session. Sometimes it is appropriate to sign an agreement for implementing the solution. In cases such as this one, it is appropriate to fill out a report form indicating how the conflict was resolved.

*"I am glad we have resolved this conflict successfully. When you were both able to sit down and talk through the problem, you were able to combine your information and to come up with the solution. You both won. Mike, you got your notes back and you learned that it would be wiser not to let them out of your sight. Juan, you found your back pack and you learned something about how it feels to lose something of value.*

*"Should anyone ask about what happened, remember to simply say that the problem has been resolved. Before you leave, please sign this report form for our records. Thank you both. I appreciated your cooperation."*

## Summary

This overview has been presented to give you a basic framework for mediating a conflict. Review the materials in the first section of this book on conflict resolution. Keep those concepts fresh in your mind. They will help you identify the nature of the conflict and give you some clues as to ways you might proceed to help resolve it.

In the final chapter we will make a few additional observations about the mediation process and your role as a peer mediator.

## Activities/Discussion

1. With the consent of all present, make a tape recording of a mediation session. Share it with your supervisor. Remember, your authority and responsibility to act as a mediator is delegated to you by your school or organization through your supervisor.

2. Keep a log of your mediating sessions. Which types of conflicts are most prevalent? What might be done in your school to prevent some of these conflicts from occurring?

# 12

# Additional Thoughts on Mediation

*"I've got my first mediation session this afternoon. There is so much to remember. I'm not sure I can be effective."*

Finally the time has come for you to put your mediation skills into action. Although you have probably role played the mediation process many times in training, dealing with an actual conflict is different. Share your successes and your fears with your supervisor as soon as possible following your session.

Here are some final thoughts concerning conflict resolution and mediation.

## The enemy of mediation—apathy

Earlier we talked about opposites. Psychologist Rollo May once said, "The opposite of love is not hate, it is apathy." People seldom invest energy in interacting with others they do not like. If there are strong feelings between two people, chances are there is life in that relationship. The conflict is worth resolving; the relationship is worth preserving.

## Competition is not the enemy

It is good to start a mediation session with the individuals in competition with each other. As they express their positions, you can get a reading on their understanding of and commitment to their individual goals.

It is important that the individuals maintain their basic aspirations at a high level to motivate them to achieve their goals. Do not be in a hurry to reach a solution. If their aspirations collapse in a rush to reach an agreement, the solution that results might be distasteful and inappropriate to both.

The obvious solution that can be reached by compromise is inferior to what can be achieved if you utilize the combined talents of all to find a solution. Sometimes you need to rekindle their competitive spirits in order to clear the air and reestablish their individual identities and aspirations. Don't fear competition; manage the energy it produces to obtain the best solution.

Educational Media Corporation®

# Working together to resolve the conflict

**Feelings.** Both have feelings. It is difficult to communicate when you feel angry, hurt, or frightened. Acknowledge the feelings of anger, frustration, and hurt on the part of both individuals. Treat everyone's feelings with respect.

**Respect.** Communicate what you feel and what you want in non-threatening language. Use caring language. Put-downs and threats cause conflicts to escalate and breed feelings of hostility and revenge.

**Define the problem.** How you define a problem or situation helps to determine how you will approach it. Identify the problem and don't lose this focus. Don't get distracted by other things and people who have nothing to do with the problem.

Both individuals own the problem. Both must work together to resolve it. Look for a win/win situation where you can solve the problem in an environment of trust and respect. The win/win strategy is a useful way to view conflict resolution because it places both on an equal standing to resolve the conflict so both win.

**Avoid paranoia.** Remind both individuals not to be paranoid. No one is out to get them. Someone once said, "If you know how little (how seldom) people thought of you, you wouldn't be so concerned." Just because you are in conflict with someone, it doesn't mean that person is your enemy. Perceive the person with whom you have a conflict as a friend, not an enemy.

**Attack the problem.** Attack the problem, not the person. Listen with an open mind. Both individuals have a point of view. Neither is 100% right. (What is the other side of the story?) Name calling and blaming don't help.

**Brainstorm.** Brainstorming is an effective technique to generate alternative solutions to a conflict. After the problem has been defined, a question like the following is asked, "What could we do in this situation?" The participants throw out as many ideas as possible without discussing or criticizing them. The atmosphere should be absolutely non-judgmental. Accept all of the ideas without comment.

No matter how wild or unusual an idea is, it may be a springboard to a new and creative way of looking at the situation. Record the ideas; organize them by placing them in categories; simplify the list; and finally, evaluate them. Discuss and develop the ideas which seem most useful.

**Offer choices.** Think of as many ways as you can to solve the problem. Allow both individuals a way out so they do not lose face in front of their peers. When a person is cornered with no alternative, this leaves no choices but to attack, withdraw with unresolved hostility, or get even.

**Modify suggestions.** After others have offered their suggestions, you might want to add a possibility or two of your own for consideration. When you have two possibilities on the table and little movement toward a solution, you might ask each participant, "Which of the two ideas proposed do you find the most acceptable?"

When one of the participants objects to a particular proposal made by another, you might ask, "How would you change this proposal to make it more acceptable?" Avoid asking, "Why did you....?" Instead, have them state what happened and how they feel about it.

**Choose and act.** Together, choose a fair solution and try it. Remember, both have the problem and both have the responsibility of solving it fairly.

## Influence, resistance, and manipulation

Use your *influence* wisely. Your influence is your ability to get others to behave in a particular way or to carry out certain actions. Overcome *resistance*. Resistance is the psychological force which keeps someone from accepting ideas and suggestions from others.

Avoid *manipulation*. Manipulation is the shrewd management or control of others, especially in an unfair or dishonest way, for you own purposes.

Mediation works best when your influence is based upon competence, expertise, and relevant information—not upon authority or popularity. Model the behaviors you want others to use.

## Positive perceptions lead to positive results

When you believe in yourself and expect to succeed, generally you will succeed. Where your expectations are negative, negative performance follows. Expect a positive result and you get it.

Expect that each person with whom you will work is capable of behaving, cooperating, and benefiting from mediation. When you act on this belief, you evoke positive behaviors in others. Focus on and expect the positive.

## Be kind to yourself.

In our attempts to help others, we sometimes inflict a subtle form of punishment upon ourselves called stress. Stress is the result of pressure, overwork, and excessive expectations. When you are tense and burdened, it is hard to act in a caring way. Take a minute several times a day and ask, "Is there something I can do to take better care of my self at this moment?" As you try this technique, you may begin to feel less pressured, more relaxed with others. Treating yourself lovingly and you spread the positive feeling to those around you.

## Summary

People seldom invest energy in a relationship with someone they do not like. The mediation session often begins with people in competition with each other, expressing their positions and strengthening their aspirations. If individual aspirations remain at a high level during the mediation process, a mutually satisfying solution will more than likely result.

Respect for feelings and positions should prevail throughout mediation. Ownership in the problem is shared; a win/win solution is sought. Attack the problem and take action on an acceptable solution.

Peer mediators have influence. This influence should be based on competency and relevant information. Your influence should never be used to manipulate others. Influence can be used to overcome the resistance of others to suggestions and ideas.

Peer mediators should take care of themselves, maintaining their own positive self-concepts in stress-producing situations.

# Request for Peer Mediation

Date _____

Individuals involved in the conflict:

_____ Grade _____

_____ Grade _____

_____ Grade _____

_____ Grade _____

Briefly describe the situation:

_____

_____

_____

_____

Person requesting mediation:

_____

Have all of the persons involved agreed to mediation?

❏ yes        ❏ no

Mediator assigned: _____

Mediation scheduled:

    Date _____ Time _____

    Place _____

Educational Media Corporation®

# Conflict Resolution Agreement

Peer Mediator _____ Date _____

How the conflict was defined:

_____

_____

_____

## Commitment to Action

I, _____, agree to _____

_____

_____

_____
(Signature)

I, _____, agree to _____

_____

_____

_____
(Signature)

Witnessed by _____
(Mediator's signature)

# Six-Inch Square Activity

Prepare for this activity by cutting 5 six-inch squares of heavy paper or cardboard according to the designs below. Number the pieces as indicated. Place all of the pieces with the same number in an envelope and number the envelopes.

The purpose of this activity is to demonstrate the need for cooperating with others to achieve common goals. As you can see from the patterns, the pieces *will* go back together into 5 six-inch squares. However, as the participants work with their pieces and the pieces they are *given* by others, some will complete their squares and others will be left with pieces that will *not* make a square. There is usually a breakthrough in this non-verbal exercise when someone breaks the rules, grabs pieces from others, or becomes frustrated with others' inability to perceive the solution. You will learn a great deal about those in your group from observing their behavior during this activity.

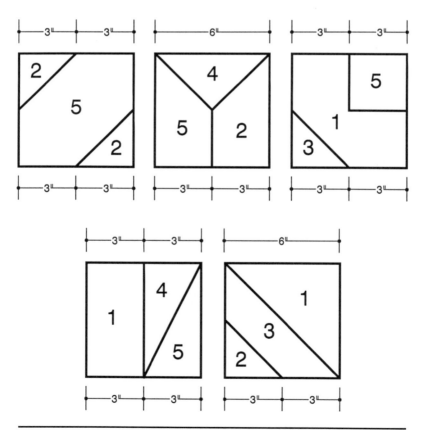

Educational Media Corporation®